50 THINGS TO DO IN THE URBAN WILD

Published by
Princeton Architectural Press
202 Warren Street
Hudson, New York 12534
www.papress.com

Published in agreement with
Pavilion Books Company Ltd.
43 Great Ormond Street
London WC1N 3HZ

ISBN 978-1-64896-154-0

For Princeton Architectural Press:
Editors: Rob Shaeffer and Stephanie Holstein
Cover design: Paul Wagner

Special thanks to Anna Houston for her feedback
and expertise on chickens.

Library of Congress Control Number:
2021947224

IMPORTANT SAFETY NOTICE
This book includes activities and projects that inherently
include the risk of injury or damage. We cannot guarantee
that following the activities or projects in this book
is safe for everyone. For this reason, this book is sold
without warranties or guarantees of any kind, expressed
or implied, and the publisher and the author disclaim
any liability for injuries, losses and damages caused in
any way by the content of this book. The publisher and
author urge the reader to thoroughly review each activity
and to understand the use of all tools before beginning
any project. Always check that you have permission to
use the land where the activities or projects take place.
Children should always be supervised when undertaking
any activity or project in this book.

50 THINGS
TO DO IN THE
URBAN WILD

Clare Gogerty

Illustrated by Maria Nilsson

PRINCETON ARCHITECTURAL PRESS · NEW YORK

Contents

Introduction

If you've ever sat at your computer at work and stared out of the window at a distant tree, or watched clouds floating past a full moon, or put sunflower kernels out for the birds, you will recognize a familiar yearning for the wild. This hunger for nature is harder to satisfy if you live in an urban area. We travel to work on a bus, sit at a desk in an air-conditioned office all day, pop out for a hasty prepackaged sandwich at lunchtime, and buy food in supermarkets on the way home. Some of us live in apartments with no outside space on streets with no trees. Many have never grown their own food and cannot recognize birdsong. Seasons come and go unnoticed.

This alienation from the natural world is not how we are meant to live. Fortunately, we don't have to: even in the most built-up environment, nature makes its presence felt. All we have to do is let it in. This book suggests fifty ways to do exactly that.

The Pull of Nature

Increasing numbers of us live in urban areas. At the time of writing, this figure is around 55 percent of the world's population and, according to the United Nations, is forecasted to rise to 68 percent by 2050. As cities, towns, and suburbs grow more congested and as green areas are eroded by development, it is more important than ever to recognize the value of what nature remains, not just for the sake of animal and plant life, but for our own well-being and happiness.

The pull of nature was particularly strong during lockdown. Birdsong grew louder as there was less noise to compete with, wild animals reclaimed quiet streets, and everyone searched for green spaces in which to take their daily walk. More than ever, we realized that immersing ourselves in the natural world should not be an occasional outing but a constant state of being.

Rethinking the Urban Landscape

The secret to connecting with nature in cities is to value what nature survives—even thrives—there and to not dismiss our urban spaces as barren, concrete jungles. Then we can build upon what we find and green up our cities for everyone to enjoy and appreciate. This may take a little mental recalibration on our part: rather than seeing urban plants as weeds, it is time to think of them as food sources for pollinators and feeding stations for caterpillars and invertebrates, and to realize that their root systems are microhabitats for various creatures that in turn are food for birds and mammals. Instead of seeing wild animals such as pigeons, raccoons, and gulls as pests to be at best tolerated and at worst culled, we should think of them as opportunists who have adapted to survive in difficult, messy circumstances and appreciate their resilience.

On Our Doorstep

Fortunately, as nature's role in our well-being and happiness is recognized, conservationists and some city planners are doing their best to make built-up areas more nature-friendly. Tree-planting programs and wildflower-rich roadsides are restoring the balance to the inner (and outer) city. Nature reserves, wetlands, and parks provide habitats for numerous creatures, and community projects enable residents to grow their own produce.

There is plenty that we can do as individuals to bring a little bit of wilderness into our lives. Whether it's the simple act of picking up a leaf, getting up early to listen to the dawn chorus, or going for a swim in a lake, it's all out there, often in unexpected places, waiting to be discovered. It only takes a willingness to find it and a few steps from the front door for nature to reveal itself.

Be an Urban Naturalist

Even in the most built-up or congested environments, nature still makes its presence felt. A wildflower pushes its way through a crack in the pavement; birds roost in derelict buildings; insects reclaim a pile of wood; moths settle on your laundry out to dry overnight on the line; and leaves tumble from city trees. By switching on your powers of observation and recording what you find, you begin to tune in to the natural world all around you, often springing up in surprising places. By increasing your awareness, you learn more about the wild world that runs parallel to the built environment, and you can gather data that will potentially help conservationists preserve what you find.

1

Hang Out with Moths

City dwellers often associate moths with the ones that lay eggs in and munch through your sweaters (these are *Tinea pellionella*, the case-bearing clothes moth, or *Tineola bisselliela*, the webbing clothes moth, both around ½ in. (1 cm) long and a dusty yellow color). This does the species a disservice, however, as there are many other types of moths out and about in the urban environment doing valuable pollination work.

Moths are most active at night, especially during warmer weather, when they emerge looking for food. Unfortunately, moth numbers have declined by almost a third in recent years, many as casualties of increasing light pollution, so it's more important than ever to monitor and record those that remain. And it is totally worth it. You can attract them by leaving a porch light on, but a simple trap is a more reliable way to lure them in. Then you will be able to study their exquisite and varied markings before recording what you find.

How to Safely Trap and Observe Moths

Moths are attracted to light and sugar. Various moth traps are available for purchase, including ones that are made up of a light, a funnel, and a container. This sugar method, however, is incredibly simple (and very effective).

Overcast, humid summer nights are best for mothing—you don't want to do it when rain or wind is in the forecast. Avoid touching the moths: their wings are fragile and easily damaged. They will fly away when they are full.

You will need: A bottle of cheap red wine, 2 lb. 3 oz. (1 kg) sugar, and a few 40 in. (1 m) lengths of cloth.

1. Mix the wine and sugar in a saucepan and heat gently until the sugar has dissolved. Let the mixture cool.

2. Soak the lengths of cloth in the sugary liquid.

3. Hang the cloths over branches, a washing line, or the back of a chair —whatever you have handy.

4. Wait for a few hours after dark, then go out and check your trap.

5. Take pictures of any moths that have landed and record what you observe in a notebook.

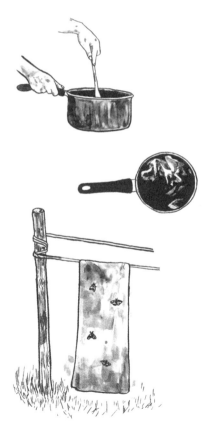

Four Common Moths of North America

Milkweed tussock moth: Along with monarch butterflies, this moth loves munching on the leaves of the milkweed. It is also known as the milkweed tiger moth because the tufts of hair of its larvae are black, white, and orange.

Gypsy moth: This invasive moth has seriously altered acres of woodland by feeding on the leaves of oak, maple, and pine trees. The female gypsy moth lays its eggs under loose bark and in a single mass—each mass containing up to one thousand eggs!

Snowberry clearwing moth: Sometimes called the "flying lobster" due to its stocky body, this pollinator hovers in front of flowers to drink their nectar. Unfurling its straw-like tongue, it can reach deep into the flower where other insects cannot reach.

Isabella tiger moth: The larva of this moth is brown in the middle and black at either end, and many believe that the length of its black ends can predict the harshness of winter. The shorter the black ends, the milder the winter!

How to Attract Moths

Plant a mixture of caterpillar-feeding plants such as nettles and cabbages, and nectar-rich, evening-scented plants for the adult moths (such as heliotrope, viburnum, salvia, foxglove, and honeysuckle). Leave piles of leaves for them to shelter in, and don't use pesticides or herbicides as they can harm moths.

Become a Citizen Scientist

One of the most valuable ways to monitor plant and animal populations in cities and towns is to become a citizen scientist. Citizen science is research carried out by non-scientists, often through smartphone apps. iNaturalist, a joint initiative between the California Academy of Sciences and the National Geographic Society (inaturalist.org), is one such app. Users photograph and identify plant species around the world, the results of which are then shared with other users and aids ongoing scientific research. The Arbor Day Foundation (arborday.org) and eBird (ebird.org) are two of many other organizations worth checking out.

Bring on the BioBlitz

To start your research, concentrate on one small patch of ground beneath your feet in a park or garden and investigate it thoroughly. You may be surprised to find it hosts an incredible number of different living species. The most popular and effective way to record these is to take part in a BioBlitz. This growing international movement encourages you to select a specific location and conduct an intensive field study.

Over a limited amount of time (usually twenty-four hours), volunteers, guided by experts, record every living thing that occupies that space. An urban area can be as rich in species as a country field, and a thorough, focused search in a park, wetland, or nature reserve is an exciting and rewarding way to spend a day.

Although you could do a BioBlitz yourself in the back garden, you will learn more at an organized event. Armed with a clipboard, species identification checklist, magnifying glass, camera, and sweep nets, you will join other wildlife enthusiasts and experts on a fascinating and valuable quest. By the end of the day, together you will have a complete snapshot of the animal and plant life found in your designated patch, creating useful data to be shared with research botanists, entomologists, and taxonomists.

Tip: To get a closer look at plants and insects, consider investing in an inexpensive 10x magnifying glass. It will open up a new and beautiful world and help you identify what you see.

Make a Field Recording

In the city, we are constantly bombarded with noise. Ignoring the cacophony of sound that engulfs us daily can feel like a matter of survival. Noise is a nuisance, something to be ignored or drowned out with a pair of headphones and a podcast. However, there are other noises out there worth listening to and recording. Birdsong, of course, but also the sound of the wind in the trees or the hoot of an owl at night.

With a recording app or simple tape recorder switched on, your ears will prick up, alert to interesting wildlife noises you may not otherwise have noticed. These field recordings are a valuable record of what you experienced on that day and a useful resource for scientists.

For inspiration, check out the National Park Service Sound Gallery (nps.gov/subjects/sound/gallery), which includes wildlife and insect recordings. For soundscape recordings of thunderstorms, rain falling on a tin roof, and a symphony of croaking frogs, go to the Sounds Archives at the British Library (sounds.bl.uk).

3

Create a Leaf Journal

Have you ever wandered along a tree-lined street or strolled
through a leafy city square and wondered what the trees around
you are called? If so, a leaf journal could be the answer. Collect
a few good leaf specimens on your travels and place them
between the pages of a book so they remain undamaged on your
way home. Then save and identify the leaves by either (or both)
of the methods on the next page. The more leaves you gather
and save, the greater your arboreal knowledge will be

OAK

MAPLE

GINGKO

Make a Leaf Rubbing

1. Place a leaf beneath a piece of paper (printer paper is fine).

2. Take a crayon and rub over the leaf evenly, making sure to include the outline so the shape is clearly defined. This works really well with large or distinctively shaped leaves such as maple, oak, and ginkgo.

3. Paste the leaf rubbing in your journal.

4. Research the tree. Write your findings beneath the leaf rubbing so you can refer to it later. Questions to ask could include: Is it deciduous? Does it have berries? What color are its leaves in autumn? What does the bark look like? How tall does it grow? How long does it live? You could also research folklore, poetry, or songs associated with that particular tree.

Make a Leaf Press

Preserve leaves by pressing them between pieces of paper. This process absorbs moisture, leaving behind a dried specimen, and is used by botanists, who catalog plants in this way before arranging them systematically in herbaria, so you will be in good company

1. Cut a small piece of cardboard into two equal halves. Take a similarly sized sheet of paper and fold in half.

2. Place the leaf, or leaves, in the fold of the paper.

3. Place the paper between the sheets of cardboard. Secure horizontally and vertically with rubber bands.

4. Leave under a stack of heavy books. When all the moisture is removed and the leaf is dry, add it to your journal with accompanying notes for future reference. This press can also be used for cut flowers.

4

Make a Rain Gauge

Some days it feels like the rain never stops, hurtling down
drains and swooshing around your feet. On other days,
light showers barely seem to dampen the pavement. But do you
know how much rain has actually fallen? It can be harder to
tell in a town or city. There is less evidence—no muddy
fields and fewer flooded rivers and lakes to monitor—
so the results can be surprising.

The urban landscape also affects rainfall. It is often the case that more rain falls in the city than in the surrounding rural and suburban areas. This is caused by the city's warmer temperatures, which causes the air to rise, then cool, forming rain-producing clouds in the process. Wind traveling around skyscrapers and through alleyways is chaotic, eventually building up and pushing warmer air into the cooler area above, where it also forms rain clouds.

Meteorologists and hydrologists use a rain gauge to measure rainfall, and you can too with this easy-to-make version. Consider making two, placing one gauge in the city and one in the nearby countryside to compare rainfall on a single day.

You will need:

An empty plastic bottle

Four cubes of jelly (made up according to instructions on the packet, but still runny)

Masking tape

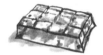

Scissors

Pencil

Ruler

1. Using the scissors, cut around the bottle about one third of the way down. Keep both parts.

2. Pour the jelly into the bottom of the bottle and allow it to set. This weighs the bottle down and creates a flat surface.

3. Turn the top part of the bottle upside down and position inside the bottom part so that it forms a funnel. Secure with the tape.

4. Mark a scale in inches or centimeters on a piece of tape and stick lengthwise to the side of the bottle.

5. Position the gauge outdoors, preferably in the middle of a garden away from trees. You want it to collect as much rain as possible. If you can, dig a hole and bury the gauge so that only the top is sticking out of the ground. This will prevent it being disturbed or blown away in the wind.

6. Check the amount of rainfall every day at the same time and record the results. Empty the bottle each time.

Build a Weathervane

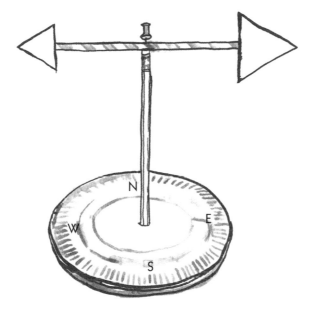

The wind that blows through a city is different to the wind that blows across a field of wheat or over a hill. Buildings in the city—often tall and rectangular with sharp edges—create obstructions not found in nature. As a result, urban winds have lower speeds and higher turbulence, especially at the base of skyscrapers, where downdrafts create strong gusts.

You will be aware of the wind as you make your way along city streets or up the road to your home or office, but it is difficult to understand exactly what it is doing. One way to make the movement of the wind visible is to build a weathervane. It's also a useful tool to help you get to know your local weather patterns as it reveals the wind's direction by pointing directly toward where the wind is coming from.

You will need: Two paper plates, small stones, cardboard, a straw, a pencil with an eraser, modeling clay, a marker, a thumbtack, scissors, and glue.

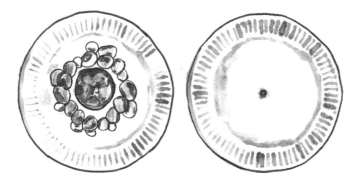

1. Make the base. Turn one paper plate upside down and make a small hole in its center. Place an egg-sized piece of modeling clay in the middle of the other plate. Flatten slightly and surround with small stones. Glue the plates together.

2. Cut one 3 in. (8 cm) equilateral triangle and one 4 in. (10 cm) equilateral triangle from the piece of cardboard.

3. Write N, S, E, and W at four points equally distanced around the edge of the paper plate base with your marker.

4. Cut small slits in both ends of the straw.

5. Insert one side of the larger triangle into one end of the straw (forming the tail of the arrow) and one side of the smaller triangle into the other end (forming the arrow's tip).

6. Insert the sharp end of the pencil through the hole in the paper plate and into the modeling clay.

7. Find the center of the straw arrow and attach it to the pencil eraser with the thumbtack. (See the illustration on page 23 for the finished weathervane.)

8. Place the weathervane where it will catch the wind. Align the compass points on the base with the correct cardinal directions, using a compass, if necessary.

9. Watch the arrow move in the wind. It will point to the direction from which the wind blows.

6

Identify Trees in Winter

Without their leaves, trees in winter have a skeletal beauty that equals their summer showiness. Lovely they may be, but they are harder to identify. The trees that line an avenue in a city center or rustle overhead in a park in summer become anonymous when they shed their leaves. There are the obvious clues to identify them, of course; the outline and bark of an oak are very different than those of a birch, but how can you be sure that that maple is not an ash when there are no leaves to guide you? Identifying deciduous trees in winter is a useful skill to have, especially as some can be without their leaves for almost half the year.

Fortunately, the clues are there when you know where to look. Most importantly, what do the buds look like? Are they round and fat, or slim and pointed? What shape, size, and color are they and what is their position on the branch—do they sit opposite each other or are they staggered? Are the twigs round or slightly flattened? Do they have leaf scars or thorns? Some trees retain fruit for the entire winter—another giveaway. Bark also varies from tree to tree—some are rough, others smooth. Finally, look at the ground around the tree to spot fallen leaves and fruit for clues.

Additional Clues to Identify a Tree

Are the buds large and sticky and opposite each other on the twig? If so, the tree is a horse chestnut.

Are the buds furry and alternate on the twig? If so, the tree is a magnolia.

Are the buds clustered at the tip of the twig? If so, it is an oak.

Does the tree have symmetrical winged fruit? If so, it is likely a maple. If they are hanging down in clusters, it is an ash.

Look at the trunk. Is the bark peeling? If so, the tree is likely to be a birch or sycamore.

Is the bark gray and smooth? If so, the tree is an alder.

Does the tree have cylindrical clusters of flowers, or catkins? If so, the tree is a birch.

7

Follow the Tracks

You may have heard rustling in the bushes during the night, but do you know what creature is out there? One way to reveal its identity is to capture the animal's tracks with a footprint trap. This could be as simple as a baking tray filled with sand left somewhere it won't be disturbed on a rain- and wind-free night. While there may not be as many species afoot as in rural areas (chances of a badger entering your tracker are slim, for example), there are still plenty of other animals out there.

Make a Weatherproof Tracker

1. Fold a piece of poster board into a triangle of three equal vertical sections.

2. Punch holes along the two edges, lengthwise.

3. Insert a piece of white paper inside the tracker.

4. Add a small amount of wet cat or dog food in dollops along the length of the paper.

5. Fasten the edge together by inserting cable ties through the holes and fixing.

6. Leave in a sheltered location— alongside a hedge, wall, or fence where it won't be disturbed is ideal.

7. Return in the morning and see who has left visible paw prints in the cat or dog food. Some possibilities are opposite.

Cat
One central pad with four uniform
smaller pads that resemble jelly beans.

Dog
Large central pad with four smaller
pads, often with claw marks.

Fox
The same number of pads as a
dog, but much narrower.

Hedgehog
Three pads point forward from
a central pad and two go out
to the sides.

Squirrel
Four toes extending from a
central pad. Its hind feet are
larger than its front feet.

Rat
While the rat has four-toed
front paws, their back paws
have five toes (shown above).

Try Tweeting and Twitching

Fortunately, birds thrive in urban environments. Good
at adapting, they are not bothered by traffic or bright lights
and make the city streets their home. Although many are
found in green spaces such as parks, around lakes, and in
cemeteries, others nest in buildings and gardens, bringing
a bit of the wild right to our doorsteps.

Once you've identified one bird, you'll want to know others.
And there are plenty for the urban birder to spot. According to
Audubon, 20 percent of avian species worldwide can be found
in cities. There are common varieties such as pigeons, starlings,
goldfinches, and blackbirds (although starling numbers are
dropping at an alarming rate), along with the more glamorous
showstoppers, such as peregrine falcons (which are happy nesting
on high, cliff-like buildings, shown opposite), American kestrels,
and sparrowhawks. Here's how to get to know them.

Feed Them Regularly

Feed birds outside your home (see page 92) and you will be able to study them closely on a daily basis. Once you have started to feed birds, it's important not to stop—they will come to depend on you for a regular source of food.

Go and Find Them

1. Get out to your local park, reservoir, cemetery, riverside, or anywhere birds gather.

2. Sit down and watch their movements, preferably with a pair of binoculars.

3. Tune your ears so that you recognize different songs and calls. Unlike many man-made sounds, birdsong is "stochastic," or made up of lots of notes that cannot be predicted. Unlike a dreaded earworm, there are no repeating patterns to focus on and it won't get stuck in your head for eternity. This creates a state where the body relaxes and the mind is alert. Listening to birdsong is, of course, also an uplifting and transporting thing to do. As bird populations decline, their songs are some of nature's most valued sounds. Fortunately, there are still plenty of places in cities and towns where birds gather in noisy communication.

4. Return to the same place and see if the same birds are there or if they have been joined by others.

5. Record the names, numbers, and habitat and you will be well on your way to becoming a full-on urban twitcher.

9

Go on a Night Safari

Even in the city, there is a whole world of wild wonder going on outdoors as we sleep. As our vision fades with the darkness, nocturnal creatures stir. One evening, resist the comforts of the sofa and go on a night safari. During the day, work out your route and locate a safe place to park yourself for potential wildlife spotting. Keep an eye out for any animal tracks or droppings that could indicate their presence. As night falls, pull on a hat and gloves to cover yourself up, let your eyes adjust to the darkness (the brightness of a flashlight may startle animals), and set off.

Owl

Owls are nocturnal, so night is when you will see them. In North America, the great horned owl is known to take up residence in trees in some urban areas.

Fox

Foxes are active at dusk and during the night when they are out searching for food. More and more they choose to live in urban areas, so chances of seeing one are good. Cubs are born in March and are fending for themselves by summer, emerging in the early evening.

Bat

Emerging from their roost site at dusk, bats flutter around for a couple of hours, looking for insects to eat. Bats do well in cities: big brown and little brown bats have been spotted in New York, living in nooks and crannies of buildings, whereas eastern red, hoary, and silver-haired bats prefer to rest in city trees.

Deer

Although not strictly nocturnal, deer are often active at night, especially in the twilight hours when it is quieter and they feel safer. You are most likely to spot mule or white-tailed deer out looking for food, especially along the outskirts of the city.

Moth

See page 11 for tips on how to attract moths to your garden.

Camera I Spy

Night cameras with infrared LEDs have built-in sensors triggered by movement and capture what the human eye cannot. Create an enticing habitat in your garden—a log pile or a pool are good options—and the wildlife will come. Set up your camera nearby and wait. Some cameras will alert your mobile phone when there is action, so all you have to do is open one eye and click.

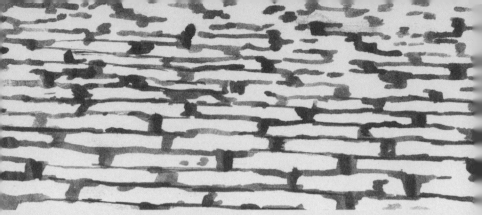

Engage with the Elements

Living and working in the city distances us from the elements.
We commute from central-heated homes in a car or by train to
air-conditioned offices, hermetically sealed from the elements.
While this has much to recommend it in terms of safety and comfort,
it also means we continue to distance ourselves from the natural
world. Taking time to swim outdoors, walk barefoot in mud, sail on
windswept water, or forage for food reconnects us with what we have
lost. Fortunately, there are plenty of ways and places to do this, even if
you live in an urban jungle rather than a rural one.

Swim Outdoors

Once you've swam outdoors and experienced its chilly thrills,
you won't want to set foot in a stuffy indoor pool again.
It is an invigorating experience at any time of the year.
In summer, you will feel the sun on your skin as you slip into
the refreshing water, and in winter, once the shock of the
cold vanishes and you strike out into the depths, you will
be rewarded with a tingling sense of well-being.

Happily, wild swimming isn't just for country dwellers. There
are many urban open water swimming destinations to discover.

City Docks and Quays
Once polluted with industrial waste, many docks have
been cleaned up and are popular open water swimming spots.
The water is tested regularly, pontoons allow easy access,
there are changing facilities, and some offer wetsuit hire and
have cafés. Go for an independent dip, join a class,
or sign up for a swim challenge.

Lakes and Ponds in Parks
With lifeguards, changing rooms, and cafés offering post-dip
mugs of hot chocolate, a swim in a park pond or lake is wild
swimming made safe and (relatively) comfortable. You may well
be accompanied by ducks paddling along at eye level. Plus
there is the option of lying in the sun on a grassy bank
post-swim with an ice cream.

Tidal Pools
Many coastal towns have pools, either natural or man-made, that
remain filled with seawater when the tide has gone out. Shallow
and sheltered, they are a safe place to swim, with the added
advantage of being close to local facilities (toilets and cafés).

Open Water Swimming Safety

Most outdoor swimming locations in cities are pretty safe, with lifeguards, plenty of other swimmers, and facilities such as showers and toilets. Should you swim in wilder water, like a tidal pool or a deserted lake, however, there are certain things to bear in mind.

1. Wear a wetsuit. It won't prevent the shock of plunging into cold water, but it will help you stay warmer for longer and keep you afloat.

2. Don't jump in. Enter the water slowly to prevent "cold water shock" and keep your face out of the water until you have your breathing under control.

3. Swim with other people.

4. When you get out of the water, dry yourself thoroughly and get dressed immediately. Put on a hat and gloves. This prevents "afterdrop," when cold blood from the extremities starts to circulate through your body again, lowering your core temperature.

5. Make sure someone knows where you are and what you are doing, and that you can be seen in the water (wear a brightly colored swimming cap).

11

Be an Urban Cowboy

Urban life distances us from animals. Apart from our pets and birds on the feeder outside the window, contact with other creatures is minimal. This is why mounting a horse, feeling its bulk and movement beneath you, and learning to communicate with it is such a powerful way to reconnect with the animal world. Fortunately, horseback riding is not confined to country lanes and windswept beaches.

Before the arrival of the automobile, when horses were the primary means of transport, the clip-clop sound of a horse on a city street was commonplace. Now the only people seen riding through the city center are mounted police. Unless, that is, you go to an urban riding school or equestrian center. Often located near open country or a large area of parkland, they offer lessons to all ages.

Here you will learn the skills necessary to keep on top of this animal, which is often ten times bigger than you. Most offer riding boots, hats, and body protectors to borrow, so there's no need to invest in any equipment straight away. Look out for introductory sessions if you're not sure if horseback riding is your thing. Once you feel convinced and have mastered the necessary skills, you will experience a sense of achievement and a feeling of freedom rare in the midst of an urban sprawl. And the horse will be your new best friend.

Get on Your Bike

Cycling in an urban environment does not necessarily need to be about weaving between buses and taxis to get to work. Bike paths and routes along traffic-free towpaths through parks offer a great way to explore and discover new areas while clearing your head and getting a nature hit. Invest in a decent bike and you could travel farther, heading out of the city and into the hills and lanes of surrounding countryside. If you don't own a bike, it's easy to rent one.

Fortunately, many cities now have clearly marked cycle routes, free from potholes and the perils of a suddenly opened car door or blindsided truck drivers. The increasing popularity of bike riding has meant greater numbers of cyclists in urban environments and growing awareness by car drivers. Join others, stay alert, and you will be able to pedal safely.

Join a Community Cycling Club

Cycling with other people is a great way to start. It will encourage you to get on your bike more often and, as a result, become healthier. It is also a way to meet other people and, as your confidence grows, you can plan expeditions to explore the wilder parts of your community.

Find an Urban Bike Park

Offering trails through parks and woodland, urban bike parks are a good option for mountain bikers wanting a bit more rough and tumble from their ride.

Share a Bike

City bike-sharing programs store bikes in racks so that people can borrow one before returning the bike to one of the many docks in the city. This provides a handy way to get around town or head to the nearest park.

Sail in the City

Getting out onto the water in a small boat or kayak is the perfect antidote to spending hours indoors in front of a computer or television. Little beats wind clipping through a sail or the gentle lap of water against the hull of a boat to revive dulled spirits. And it's not restricted to coastal areas: the popularity of recreational sailing means that many sailing clubs now operate on city reservoirs, rivers, harbors, and lakes. (Cities by the sea have entire oceans as their playground.)

To learn sailing basics, head to a city sailing club. Try an introductory class and you will soon be out on the water in a dinghy, managing sails, wind, and currents like a pro. Deepen your skills and learn how to navigate or become a competent crew member. There are lessons available for children, too, and races and regattas to put your new skills to the test.

Once a city sailor, you will find yourself gliding, the wind in your sails, as you pass familiar landmarks, the city skyline now seen in an entirely new way from the water.

Try Kayaking

Alternatively, rent a kayak or canoe and paddle along a river or canal through the heart of a city center. As your oars slice through the water and you quietly slip past riverside offices and homes, wildlife will reveal itself. Easy to learn and manage, city kayaking is a calming, meditative experience that brings you closer to nature despite being a stone's throw from the hustle and bustle of urban life.

Photograph All Four Seasons

In the city, the seasons slip from one to the next almost without us noticing. We may put on an extra layer as we leave the house, frantically look for the snow plow on a wintry morning, or joyfully put on sunglasses when the sun comes out, but it's easy to miss what is going on in nature.

Photographing the seasonal changes that occur in a designated place throughout the year is a mindful exercise that reminds us of how each season differs from the next. It encourages us to observe the subtle shifts as days lengthen and shorten and temperatures rise and fall.

1. Choose your location. Find a patch of nature near your home. This could be an area of your garden, a flowerbed in your local park, a beautiful tree by the side of the road or anything that changes with the seasons and has sufficient interest to photograph.

2. Think about timing. To get a consistent result, photograph your subject at the same time of day each season. You could choose early morning as you go to work, or lunchtime when you have time to spare. Remember that the days are short in winter; an evening shot will be dark and you may need a flash.

3. Select your shot. When you have found your subject, think of how you will frame it. Aim for a good composition, with a strong focal point that won't disappear in winter. A tree, shrub, or bird feeder, for example, would hold the image. Take multiple shots from this position, and remember where you are standing for next time.

4. Plan the frequency. You may ambitiously consider taking a picture every day. Or you may choose to shoot once a week or just once a month. Whatever you decide, be consistent— if it's once a week, keep to the same day.

5. Study the results. Once you have your record of the seasons, gather the shots and notice how each image is different. Print the images to display them, or paste them into an album for future reference.

Camp in the Garden

Pitch a tent in the garden and you have the makings of a mini adventure. Step out of your routine and life expands. Rather than dozing in front of the TV, a night under the stars means you can toast marshmallows on a campfire, warm up a can of beans on a camping stove, and spot constellations in the sky (see page 74). Instead of waking up to the sound of a noisy alarm, birdsong will interrupt your sleep as dawn breaks. You may not escape the city serenade of sirens, traffic, and neighbors chatting, but nature is not far away. Wrapped up warmly, you can watch the moon move across the sky as the fire crackles.

A backyard campout even makes rainy nights—usually the curse of the camper—romantic. Listening to the patter of rain on the tent is bearable, pleasurable even, when you know it's just for one night and you can go home in a minute if it gets to be too much. Plus there's a familiar bathroom a short distance away, and one you don't have to find with the aid of a flashlight.

All this is possible even if you have only a small patch.
Just remember to keep something handy to put the fire out
if it gets too lively—a bucket of water or a shovel will do it—
and take a cot, a good sleeping bag, and a pillow.
Camping, especially in your own garden, should be cozy.

Garden Camping Necessities

Tent: Obviously.

Cot: Essential, unless you want to wake up with a cracking headache the following morning.

Sleeping bag: Or make do with blankets and some pillows.

Firepit: A bit of a luxury, but nothing says "camping" like gathering around a flickering fire, preferably with marshmallows at the ready.

Chairs or a rug: Something to sit on, or you will get damp as the dew rises.

Solar lights or lanterns: The twinklier the better. You want to create a cozy, magical vibe.

Camping stove: If you intend to cook a meal or boil a kettle out there. However, you could just as easily head back to the kitchen.

Snacks and drinks: You need something to munch on or sip as you gaze into the fire or watch the moon rise over the city.

16

Forage for Fruit

It pays to be observant when you go for a walk in your
neighborhood. There is food everywhere if you know where to look.
Even an area of rough ground may have a tangle of blackberry
bushes, or an elderly rose plant, bursting with rose hips, scrambling
over a derelict building. Parks, recreational grounds, golf courses,
and roadsides all have plenty of fruity pickings for the urban forager.

Blackberries

These generous bushes are laden with fruit and grow everywhere. Find a good cropping one—preferably a little out of the way to avoid other foragers—and stick with it. Wear gloves to prevent your hands from being slashed by thorns, and pick enough to make a lovely cobbler.

Rose Hips

The bright red fruit of the dog rose decorates its thorny host in August. Make sure the hips are ripe before you pick them (they will be deep red), then make into a Vitamin C-rich syrup (they aren't edible in any other form). Either drink neat for a health boost or pour over pancakes or ice cream.

Sloes

While not commercially grown in the United States, sloes grow wild in some eastern states. Round, purple, and hard, this species of plum is best enjoyed (by adults) when soaked in a mixture of gin and sugar to create sloe gin. Mix equal quantities of each and try to resist drinking for a year or two, by which time the flavor will be fully developed.

Wild Plums

Smaller than those found in supermarkets, these little mouthfuls are delicious eaten raw when fully ripe, and equally tasty cooked and added to a crumble or pie. A close relative to the sloe, beach plums grow in sandy soil along the Northeast Atlantic coast.

17

Visit a Well or Spring

Even in the most built-up environment, water is never
far away. A whole world of buried hidden rivers and forgotten
streams flow under your feet. While most of these have been
diverted out of sight, some still emerge as wells and springs.
A natural spring or well is usually a modest thing bubbling
quietly from the ground or gently welling from a rock. The same
is true of city springs, which spurt unobtrusively from walls,
overlooked by busy pedestrians. Once an important source
of drinking water or a pilgrimage destination, urban natural
springs have been mostly forgotten.

City Springs and Holy Wells

A search for an urban spring or well is a rewarding one.
A large-scale map will point you in the right direction. City
springs are frequently enclosed in special architectural nooks with
inscriptions carved into the stone surrounding them. Originally
a place to find drinking water for people and their animals, many
are now neglected. Holy wells are located beside churchyards and
are dedicated to saints or pagan gods. Water was used for healing,
either by drinking or bathing in it. Both can reveal much about
local history and folklore and are well worth researching.

It's an old English custom to drop some silver into a well as
an offering. Traditionally, bent pins were used, the precedent for
throwing coins into fountains. However, it is best to respect the
site and natural surrounds, so consider leaving nothing but wishes
and gratitude. And while it is tempting to drink the water, only do
so if you know it's safe or if you have filtered it yourself.

Thermal Waters

City hot springs, which bubble more dramatically from
the ground, have become spas where office workers,
tourists, and locals soak away their anxieties. Plenty of
American and European cities have pools with thermally
heated water where it's possible to bathe outdoors at any time
of the year. Many are believed to have healthful properties
and offer a variety of treatments. Others boast different pools
at various temperatures—such as cold-water plunge pools—
and saunas. Refreshing and restorative, they are
a soothing antidote to city life.

18

Create Land Art

The next time you go for a walk in a nearby wood, beach, park, or lake, think about what you find—twigs, leaves, stones, or pebbles—as materials for a work of art. This is how land artists see the natural world. Items found on the trail are regarded as their material, the earth as their canvas. By borrowing natural things and using them to create structures directly in the landscape, artists collaborate with nature to make something new and beautiful. The art they create is ephemeral and does not damage its surroundings in any way.

Create Your Own Land Art

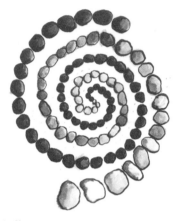

Collect pebbles or stones of a similar size and arrange in a spiral. Leave it where you found them.

Find variously colored leaves and flowers and arrange in a mandala on the forest floor.

Pick up twigs as you walk, then create a sculptural form in the landscape from what you've found.

Rake sand on a beach or foreshore into interesting patterns, then watch as the tide washes it away.

Collect small pieces of plastic litter. Wash carefully, then arrange in a flat composition. (See the work of Steve McPherson, who works with marine litter, for inspiration.)

Remember to photograph what you create!

Inspiring Land Artists

Chris Drury: Creates ephemeral work from stone, wood, and earth as well as "cloud chambers" to watch the sky through a hole in a dark cairn, or man-made pile of stones.

Andy Goldsworthy: Works with flowers, leaves, icicles, mud, snow, and twigs, among other natural materials, to make site-specific work.

Maya Lin: Uses natural materials from each project site to create her earthworks. One of these works, Wavefield, located in Storm King Art Center in New Windsor, NY, includes seven undulating hills created out of gravel and topsoil.

Richard Long: Combines earth, rock, mud, plants, and stone to create sculpture that he then documents with photography. Also bases some work upon walks undertaken through the landscape.

19

Bring Nature Indoors

If you don't have a garden, you can still have a houseplant
or two. Or several. There is room in even the smallest home
for many pots of greenery. Houseplants introduce the natural
world into your home and bring the space to life. They also
cleverly clean the air, filtering pollutants through their roots
and releasing oxygen in exchange.

The trick to keeping houseplants alive is to respect their origins. Create an environment that is in tune with their natural habitats, whether it's the rainforest, the desert, or a rocky mountainside, and they will thrive. This can be as simple as keeping them out of direct sunlight or spraying regularly with a mister. Try to avoid a single plant languishing on a shelf. Plants love company and are happiest clustered together.

Five Great First Houseplants

Fiddle-leaf Fig
A statuesque plant with broad, paddle-shaped leaves that prefers to be kept out of direct sunlight. If you have a pet at home, be mindful that this plant is toxic to them if ingested.

Spider Plant
Almost impossible to kill, the spider plant rewards even poor care with cascading offshoots that can be propagated to produce more plants.

Pothos
Its heart-shaped leaves will dangle
decoratively from the top of a bookcase
or a shelf in the kitchen or bathroom
(most houseplants love the steaminess
of a bathroom). Grows vigorously
and easily.

Chinese Money Plant
Circular leaves grow from straight stems.
Baby plants sprout at its base, making it
easy to propagate and spread the pilea
love among your friends.

Air plants
Carefree plants that grow without
a pot or any soil. A regular misting
and occasional dunking in water
will keep them happy.

20

Search the Shore

You might think that the muddy foreshore of a city river is an unlikely place to find treasure, but mudlarkers know different. These urban explorers scour the mud at low tide looking for all manner of forgotten everyday objects. Some are hundreds of years old, left behind as the tide goes out and preserved by the anaerobic nature of the mud.

The original mudlarkers were poor children who scavenged the foreshore of the River Thames in eighteenth- and nineteenth-century London looking for things like firewood, nails, rope, and bones of drowned animals to sell. These days it's all about searching for artifacts that reveal glimpses of the city's past.

It is an absorbing and rewarding activity that is a hotline to the city's social history. It also gives you the opportunity to spend time beside the river on the foreshore, listening to the lapping waves and the screech and squawk of waterfowl. Limit yourself to a mile or so of shoreline and time your search for when the tide is out. You may find something that has been untouched since it was lost or discarded hundreds of years ago.

While mudlarking is incredibly popular in London on the shores of the Thames river, groups of mudlarkers are popping up in cities around the United States. Most finds are not valuable, but all are fascinating relics of social history with a story to tell.

Popular Mudlarking Finds

Clay Pipes
Dating from the 1560s to the 1930s, pipes were often sold with packs of tobacco and discarded once used.

Clay Roof Tiles
Representative of urban architecture from a bygone era.

Fragments of Plateware
Often the distinctive blue and white Delftware, popular in the seventeenth century.

Metal Buckles
Worn on shoes and belts from the mid-seventeenth to late eighteenth century.

Buttons
Nineteenth-century work buttons
and gentlemen's suspender
buttons are common.

Keys
Dating from all ages, some
keys are clunkier than others.

Animal Bones
Leftovers from the bustling
markets near city ports.

Need to Know

All mudlarkers should check with their local officials to find out
if permits are required. It makes sense to go with a guide who has
a permit and knows where to look. Remember to wear working
boots and rubber gloves (there is a slim danger of catching rat-borne
illnesses). Keep an eye on the tide: currents can be strong and it's
easy to get stranded. Don't dig or poke in the mud, and use only
your eyes to find treasures. You can keep what you find, however,
if an item appears valuable, consider reporting what you find to
local authorities or a museum.

21

Go Barefoot

Our feet rarely see daylight, especially in the city. Usually, they are confined in socks or tights and shoes. Toes are restricted and cannot wiggle, and our nerve-rich soles are cushioned and further separated from earth. Every once in a while, it feels good to release your feet and marvel at their sensitivity and complexity. Walking barefoot is also a rare opportunity for the urban dweller to become grounded and connect with the land beneath them.

Of course, there are fewer barefoot options in the city than on a beach, say, or in a field. Pavement laden with chewing gum and gasoline-slick roads are not appealing places to walk. It's best to restrict it to a garden where you can control your environment, or a carefully chosen patch of public park. The point is to feel the earth beneath your feet and let it ground and center you; you only have to walk a few steps for this to work.

1. Find an appropriate place to walk. This can be fairly small area: the first time you might just want to stand. Grass is perfect, especially first thing in the morning when the dew hasn't evaporated. Feet love the feeling of soft, wet grass. Squelchy mud, hot rocks, and autumn leaves also work.

2. Make sure nothing nasty is lurking. You don't want to spoil the experience by treading in something unpleasant or cutting your feet on something sharp. Peel off your socks and simply stand. Notice any new sensations.

3. Walk a few steps and recognize how differently you are moving.

4. When you decide to stop, examine your feet in case of injury, give them a wipe, then pull your socks and shoes back on.

Look to the Skies

Whatever is going on around you—queues of traffic,
people jostling on the pavement, the general activity of the
city—there is always a wild, unspoiled place above your
head. The sky is a constant theater of natural attractions.
During the day, there are clouds to stare at dreamily,
birdsong to enjoy, and murmurations to marvel at (see page
80). By night, the moon and stars come out to dazzle and
bewitch. Wherever you are, the great big sky is putting on
its own spectacular show.

Cloud Spotting 101

Always above us and forever changing, no matter where you live—even in the heart of the city—clouds are a constant, fascinating presence. Get a glimpse of them between houses and shops or climb to the top of a tall building for a panoramic view. Simply staring at the sky and its shifting cloud patterns can be a calming and meditative activity. It can also give you a good idea of what weather is on the horizon. White clouds reflect light from the sun and indicate good weather, whereas gray clouds are full of water and mean rain is on its way.

Basically, clouds are masses of water droplets or ice crystals suspended in the atmosphere. They form when water vapor—which is always present in the sky—condenses. Temperature, wind, and other conditions where a cloud forms determine what type of cloud it will be. Clouds form at different levels in the atmosphere and are grouped into three categories.

CIRRUS

CIRROSTRATUS

CUMULONIMBUS

CIRROCUMULUS

ALTOCUMULUS

ALTOSTRATUS

STRATOCUMULUS

NIMBOSTRATUS

CUMULUS

STRATUS

High level
Height at base: 18,000–40,000 feet (5,500–12,000 m)

Cirrus: Thin, streaky, wispy clouds. May take on the colors of the rising or setting sun.

Cirrostratus: Thin, transparent clouds formed in layers covering large areas of the sky, sometimes thousands of miles.

Cirrocumulus: Small patchy cloudlets grouped together. Composed almost entirely of ice crystals.

Middle level

Altocumulus: *Height at base: 6,500–18,000 feet (2,000–5,500 m).* Small patchy cloudlets shaped in rounded clumps.

Altostratus: *Height at base: 6,500–20,000 feet (2,000–6,000 m).* Featureless gray layer of cloud that can conceal the sun. Usually a mixture of water droplets and ice crystals.

Low level

Stratocumulus: *Height at base: 1,200–6,500 feet (365–2,000 m).* Clumps or patches of clouds varying in color from bright white to dark gray.

Cumulus: *Height at base: 1,200–6,500 feet (365–2,000 m).* Detached puffy clouds usually spotted in good weather.

Cumulonimbus: *Height at base: 1,100–6,500 feet (335–2,000 m).* Heavy, dense clouds extending high into towers or peaks. Usually signals extreme weather, such as torrential downpours, hailstorms, thunder, and lightning.

Nimbostratus: *Height at base: 2,000–10,000 feet (600–3,000 m).* A dark and featureless layer that covers most of the sky, often accompanied by continuous heavy rain or snow.

Stratus: *Height at base: 0–1,200 feet (0–365 m).* Very low, gray layers of clouds. Sometimes appear at ground level as mist or fog.

Follow the Moon

Seen through a window, from a busy street, or above a back garden,
the Moon is always bewitching and transcendental. It is also a good
way to tune into the turning of the year and the passing of time.

The Moon is Earth's only satellite and revolves around the planet,
reflecting the light from the Sun. As the Moon orbits the Earth,
and Earth orbits the Sun, the lunar phases gradually change
as reflected sunlight falls on different parts of the Moon.

Know Your Lunar Cycles

Waxing crescent: The bright crescent appears on the right-hand side of the Moon and increases (waxes) until it becomes a full moon.

First quarter: Occurs a week after the new moon. One half of the Moon is illuminated.

Waxing gibbous: The Moon is almost completely illuminated.

Full moon: The Moon is fully illuminated. This disc of mottled brightness—sometimes silver, sometimes golden—casts a pale white light.

Waning gibbous: The illumination of the Moon begins to decrease.

Last quarter: The other half of the Moon is illuminated.

Waning crescent: The bright crescent appears on the left-hand side of the Moon and decreases (wanes) until it vanishes at the new moon.

New moon: The Moon appears to vanish as reflected sunlight hits its far side and the shadow of Earth entirely covers it.

Different Full Moons

The full moon varies in size, color, and position in the sky at different times of the year. A useful way to keep track of the year, the Moon has been used (and named) by different cultures in its various guises accordingly.

Blue moon: Each year has thirteen full moons—eleven months with one full moon and one with two—which occur every twenty-nine days or so. The second full moon in a month is called a blue moon.

Wolf moon: Occurs in January and is named after the howling of hungry wolves in midwinter.

Harvest moon: Occurs in September when crops are gathered. The Moon is particularly bright and rises early, allowing farmers to harvest into the night.

Hunter's moon: Occurs in October when fields are bare and animals have nowhere to hide from the hunter. It is a bright moon that stays in the sky for a long time.

24

Greet the Sunrise with the Dawn Chorus

Sometimes it's really worth setting the alarm and getting up early. Seeing the sun rise as the dawn chorus breaks is a good enough reason. Anyone anywhere can experience this uplifting spectacle, when massed birds break into song. It sounds just as good heard from a city balcony, doorstep, or through an open window.

The best time of the year to rise early is spring or summer, and 4:00 a.m. is the average time to catch birds in full song. It is an uplifting, joyful thing for us to hear, but for birds the dawn chorus has a purpose: they are either defending their territory or calling to attract a mate. It is thought that the birds sing as the morning breaks because it is a peaceful time of day, with no background noise to interfere with their song.

The dawn chorus is a rolling event with different species joining the sing-along at different times of day. Train your ear to recognize and differentiate the various calls and songs. Some of the most frequently heard birds include:

Blackbird
A mellow baritone song punctuated by tuneful whistles and a few high-pitched notes.

Robin
A solitary voice and one of the first as they wake early, driven by hunger to search for worms to eat. A liquid song that leaps from high notes to low and back again.

House Sparrow
Its distinctive "chip" call is repeated over and over again.

Wren
A surprisingly loud song for such a small bird. As it eats insects, the wren arrives later than robins and blackbirds.

25

Catch Sight of Constellations

The full glory of the night sky can be difficult to make out in urban
environments as street lights and pollution often obscure it. However,
it is possible to see many interesting things if you take a little care.

Tips for City Astronomers

- Find a high position, preferably above buildings—on a rooftop
  or the top of a parking garage, for instance—to minimize light
  pollution and avoid trees obstructing your line of sight.

- Take a pair of binoculars. You will be able to see the
  major constellations along with Saturn and some moons
  of Jupiter through binoculars.

- Wait for a clear, cloudless evening. Moonless winter nights are best
  (city heat in the summer generates sky-obscuring humidity and haze).

- If you are in your garden, turn off outdoor lights.

- Once you have found your spot, settle in, and let your
  eyes adjust for ten minutes or so.

The eighty-eight named constellations are constantly moving across the sky, each visible at different times of the year. The following three constellations are the easiest to see.

Orion ("the Hunter")

Where to look: The southwest portion of the sky. Find three bright stars in an almost straight vertical line at equidistance from each other. These form Orion's belt. The two bright stars above are his shoulders and a triangle of stars above make up his head. You should also be able to identify his arm, which is holding a bow.

When to see it: In the northern hemisphere, Orion is clearest in late November and early December.

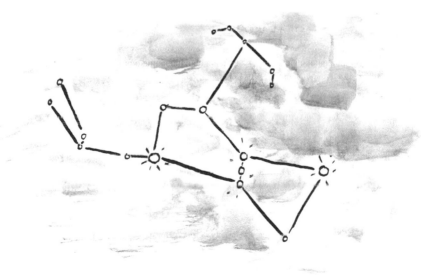

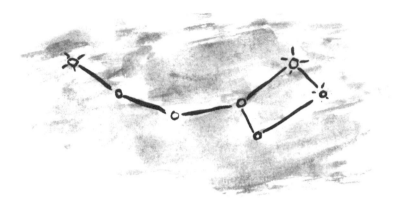

Ursa Minor ("the Little Bear")

Where to look: The northern sky, although it can be obscured by light pollution. This is a relatively small but easily recognizable constellation comprising seven bright stars shaped like a soup ladle (or "dipper"). At the end of the ladle's handle is the North Star (or Polaris), which was traditionally used as a navigational aid.

When to see it: To maximize your chances of seeing it, look to skies in June.

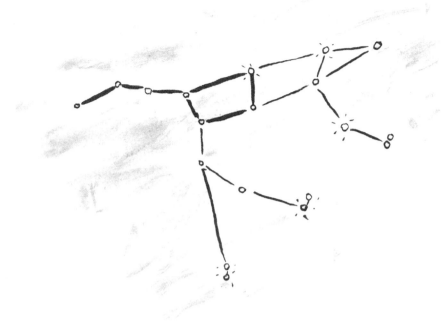

Ursa Major ("the Great Bear")

Where to look: The northern sky. Like Ursa Minor, its seven main stars resemble a soup ladle, with a cup and a handle, although a much bigger one. It has also been compared to a bear (the bowl of the ladle being the bear's rump), a plough, and a wheelbarrow. The two stars that form the bottom of the ladle point to the North Star (Polaris) at the tail of Ursa Minor.

When to see it: Ursa Major is always visible in the northern hemisphere, but the best time to see it is in spring, when it is high above the northeastern horizon.

Watch a Meteor Shower

Meteor showers are one of the night sky's greatest shows, with the big advantage that they can be seen without a telescope or when climbing a mountain. You will have to get up in the middle of the night, though, and be prepared to wait.

Meteors begin their lives as part of a comet (a frozen ball of gases, rock, and dust). As the comet orbits near the sun, some of its surface thaws and falls off. This debris burns up as it heads towards Earth, forming cascades of meteoroids. Also known as shooting stars, they flash across the sky, leaving a bright trail of glowing air as they enter Earth's atmosphere.

When to See Major Meteor Showers

Meteor showers are named after the constellation they appear to originate from. Orionids, for example, which appear in October, look as though they are falling from Orion.

Quadrantids

One of the best annual meteor showers, known for bright fireball meteors, although they are short-lived and usually over in a few hours.
Active: Late December/early January.
Look like they're coming from: The Boötes constellation, originally called Quadrans Muralis.

Lyrids (above)

One of the oldest known meteor showers: records go back almost three thousand years. Expect up to fifteen meteor showers per hour at their peak.
Active: April.
Look like they're coming from: The constellation Lyra.

Perseids (opposite)

Meteors streak brightly across the sky every couple of minutes, making this one of the most-watched showers.
Active: July and August.
Look like they're coming from: The constellation Perseus.

Orionids

Not the most visible shower, you could see up to twenty Orionids per hour at their peak just before dawn.
Active: October.
Look like they're coming from: The constellation Orion.

Leonids

Bright, colorful meteors shoot through the sky at a rate of around fifteen per hour. Traveling at around 44 miles (71 km) per second, they are considered some of the fastest meteors in space.
Active: Mid-November.
Look like they're coming from: The constellation Leo.

Geminids

Considered one of the most reliable meteor showers, with up to 120 meteors per hour visible in good conditions. Geminids are bright, fast, and yellow.
Active: Mid-December.
Look like they're coming from: The constellation Gemini.

27

Marvel at Murmurations

The mass movement of starlings (known as a murmuration) is one of nature's most jaw-dropping sights. The sight of thousands of birds swooping, wheeling, and diving, moving as one unified organism, creating beautiful shapes in the sky, is unforgettable— as is the noise they make when they fly overhead, a whooshing murmur that gives the spectacle its name.

Starlings perform this aerial display before they roost for the night. It is thought that grouping together like this keeps predators such as peregrine falcons at bay, and the body heat of that number of birds raises the air temperature and helps to keep them warm.

All North American starlings—which may total more than 200 million—are descended from roughly one hundred birds that were released in the early 1890s in New York City's Central Park.

When to See a Murmuration
Early evening, during the winter months of November and December, just before dusk. This is the peak of the starling's migration season. There's also a chance of spotting one at sunrise, as the birds set off from their roosts to fly to feeding grounds.

Where to See a Murmuration
Starlings roost in places that are sheltered from the weather and predators. In urban areas, this could mean big industrial buildings or derelict structures. You can often see starling murmurations in large open areas just outside of the city limits, as well as in parks, marshes, and woodland fields.

Make Space for Nature

In many towns and cities, nature has been elbowed out. The demands of industry, commerce, and housing have led to areas of wilderness being reduced, while the patches of nature that remain have been either destroyed or tidied up and sanitized. This is why it's important that we do what we can to help redress the balance. Gardens are a rich, biodiverse tapestry of plants, insects, and wildlife. By adding a few extra elements, we can let nature in and, once it arrives, it will thrive. Similarly, there are things we can do in outdoor public spaces that will make a world of difference.

Build for Biodiversity

All kinds of wildlife, especially flying creatures like bats and birds, are forever on the lookout for nesting and roosting sites. Unfortunately, these have become increasingly hard to find in urban areas. With a little help from us, however, they can be encouraged to hang out in our gardens, sheds, and garages, no matter how small these spaces are. Build the right structure and put it in the right place and you will provide a happy habitat for wildlife, boost biodiversity, and get a fascinating insight into animal behavior.

Bat Box

Bats are nocturnal creatures and need somewhere safe to sleep and raise their pups during the day. A bat box is an artificial roost designed to encourage them to inhabit areas where there are few roosting sites. There are many different types of bat boxes to choose from, either ready-made or to make yourself. If you choose to make one, remember to use untreated wood and make sure the joints are tight—bats are sensitive to smell and hate draughts.

Place your bat box under the eaves of your house or garage or on the trunk of a large tree, ideally 10 ft. (3 m) from the ground.

Alternatively, incorporate a bat roof tile into your roof space. This allows bats to crawl into the roost area without disturbing your house's occupants.

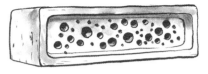

Bee Brick

The number of solitary bees is in serious decline. One of the reasons is the loss of suitable habitats for them to lay their eggs. A bee brick is essentially a brick used for building but it is shot through with holes. Bees crawl into these cavities and lay their eggs before sealing up the entrance with muck and chewed-up vegetation. When the offspring are ready to emerge the following spring, they burst through the entrance and fly away. As solitary bees have no queen or hive to protect, they are not aggressive and will not sting.

Either incorporate the brick into a wall or place it on its own in a sunny spot at least 3½ ft. (1 m) from the ground, if possible near bee-friendly plants such as honeysuckle, lavender, or buddleia.

Swallow Shelter

Swallows darting and swooping in the warm air encapsulate summer. Encourage them to continue visiting by fixing a nest platform where you would like them to nest. This could be in the eaves of your house, garage, or shed   just make sure it's out of reach of any cats. Place a plastic bag beneath the ledge to catch droppings.

29

Construct a Hedgehog Highway

Many smaller mammals, like the hedgehog and the shrew, enjoy the safety and shelter found in gardens, especially those that provide plenty to eat and places to sleep.

Some of these helpful creatures are experiencing a decline in population and the chances of seeing any in an urban setting has become unlikely. This is partly due to the fences we erect between our gardens, which frequently come with an impenetrable concrete gravel board at their base. Small mammals that cannot climb trees or fences like to roam from garden to garden, often traveling up to a mile in search of food or a mate. Enclosed gardens can trap them and foil their plans.

Happily, it is easy to correct this and create a wildlife highway linking garden to garden. Most non-climbing creatures only need a hole of 5 x 5 in. (13 x 13 cm) maximum to pass through, which is too small for most pets and can be cut out of the fence. Alternatively, if you have gravel board at the base of your fence, try digging a passage under it or installing a piece of terracotta piping as a tunnel. Best of all, pull down the fence and plant a hedge.

More Ways to Welcome Hedgehogs

- Provide shelter by leaving parts of the garden untended and gathering up leaves and wood. This will also attract invertebrates, slugs, and beetles, which small mammals like to eat.

- If you are erecting a new fence, include a panel with a ready-made hedgehog-friendly gravel board.

- Leave out food, such as tinned dog or cat food (not fish-based) and crushed dog biscuits.

- Keep them hydrated by putting out a shallow bowl of water. If you have a pond, make sure they can reach the water easily by placing stones or pebbles at its edge. Cover any open drains in case they fall in and drown.

30

Harness the Magic of Worms

There are more than 150 species of earthworms in North America, all varying in size and color and each playing their part to make our gardens grow. They do this by eating decaying plant material, digesting it, then excreting it as fertilizer. They also increase the amount of air that gets into the soil by moving through the dirt.

One way to harness the magical powers of worms is to use them to turn your kitchen waste into compost. There are many purpose-built compost wormery kits to buy that come with the right sort of worms, but you could also make your own (and buy the worms from a fishing-tackle specialist). Choose a bin small enough to sit in your backyard, within easy reach for getting rid of vegetable peelings.

You will need:

A large plastic box with a lid

Brown cardboard or newspaper

A drill

A couple of bricks

Worms (see page 91)

Compost

1. Drill holes in the bottom of the box. The more the better, within reason— you don't want so many perforations that the bottom falls through.

2. Put the box on the bricks to raise it off the ground so that it is ventilated.

3. Line the bottom of the box with cardboard or newspaper to prevent the worms from falling out.

4. Drill holes in the lid for extra ventilation.

5. Cover the bottom of the box with around 2 in. (5 cm) of compost or coir. Lightly dampen with a plant mister.

6. Add the worms. Consider brandling worms, also known as red worms, which are available in fishing tackle shops to be used as bait. You will need 300–500 worms.

7. Add kitchen waste. Stick to produce peels, teabags, and coffee grounds. Avoid adding meat, dairy, and processed foods. Supplement with shredded paper, cardboard, or wood chips. You will need to add about 25 percent of these carbon-rich materials with each load.

8. Cover everything with another layer of newspaper or cardboard and spray with water. Put the lid on.

9. Wait for the worms to work their magic. When the waste has turned to compost, leave some of the mixture in the bin to make the next batch. The compost will be rich in nutrients and may used as top dressing for pots and planters, or as a base for a potting soil when mixed with perlite.

31

Feed the Birds

Putting food out for the birds is a simple way to reconnect with nature that's available to all of us. A bird feeder placed outside a window (or stuck on the actual pane if you have no outside space) is a joyful, positive way to satisfy our yearning for a meaningful connection with nature and the wild. It provokes an intimate and profound moment of trust with a wild creature that can be hard to find in the city. We think we're feeding the birds for their sake, but more often than not, it's for us too.

Different birds have different preferences, both for food and how they find it. Some like to feed on the ground, while others prefer to search in trees. Provide a range of feeders in different sites to attract a wide variety. Remember to clean the feeders regularly so the birds don't pick up infections.

Seed Feeder
A plastic tube with metal perches that can be hung from a tree or pole. Fill with sunflower hearts and wild bird food mix to attract many different types of birds, including house sparrows, chickadees, and goldfinches. Put a seed tray beneath the feeder to catch falling seed debris.

Ground Feeder
Either sprinkle food directly on to the lawn or patio (keeping an eye out for any lurking cats) or use a ground feeding table (a raised piece of wood). It will be used by blackbirds, thrushes, wrens, and robins who prefer to feed at ground level.

Nut Feeder
A wire-mesh tube or metal tube
punctured with holes that
can be filled with peanuts or suet
nibbles and will attract woodpeckers and nuthatches.

Suet Feeder
A square metal cage to contain
blocks of suet enriched with
insects. Popular with chickadees
and starlings (who also love
mealworms).

On Feeding Birds in Public Places

It can be tempting to feed bread to the ducks and other
waterbirds in parks, or to scatter seed for pigeons and other birds
in public spaces. Be wary of this, however: it can do more harm
than good. "Human" food, which often contains high levels
of salt and sugar, can be harmful to birds. Scattered around,
it will attract large numbers of crows and magpies, which bully
and prey on smaller birds. It can also affect water quality.
Best to leave it for the parks to manage.

Grow Up
a Wall

There is no better way to attract birds, pollinators, and other insects than by growing flowering plants. Plus, you get the benefit of scented blooms, cut flowers, and all-round loveliness. This can be tricky in towns or cities, however, where personal gardens are rare. Where there's a wall there's a way, though, and if you have the itch to garden and some outdoor space, however small, there is a solution: think vertically.

Any outside wall can be covered in greenery. This has the multiple benefits of hiding ugly masonry, attracting wildlife, and greening up a dreary spot. Once established, it will provide a place for butterflies to hibernate and bees to shelter from the rain and be a source of food for a range of wildlife species.

Grow climbing plants in pots or plant beds, and guide with wires or a trellis that is firmly attached to the wall.

Five Climbing Plants Loved by Wildlife

Passion Flower
Exotic blooms on intertwining stems that provide shelter for insects and birds as well as nectar for some pollinators. Grows vigorously and will cover a wall quickly (see page 95).

Honeysuckle
The gorgeous scent of the flowers attracts moths (and other pollinators) to its nectar. Once established, it also provides shelter and delicious berries for birds.

Hops
Dies back in winter, so not good for all-year wall coverage, but during the summer it will provide shelter for insects and leaves for caterpillars, along with hops should you want to brew your own beer.

Ivy

Its rampant growth will cover a wall speedily and keep it covered all year. Birds like to nest, and insects hibernate, in ivy. Its flowers provide nectar for pollinators when there isn't much around (late autumn), followed by berries appreciated by birds including thrushes and blackbirds.

Star Jasmine

Good to plant near a door: its white flowers smell heavenly. They also attract pollinators.

Make a Green Wall

Alternatively, buy a green-wall system of pockets that you fill with compost (sold in panels at garden centers). Add extra panels as needed. Plant vertically with ferns, periwinkles, pelargoniums, and wild strawberries for a tumbling, wildlife-friendly display.

33

Green Up Your Shed, Porch, or Bike Shelter

Any flat, level surface in your outdoor space is a potential haven for pollinating insects and wild birds. Instead of a dull, gray piece of roof felt, plant a green roof on your shed, porch, or bike shelter. Watch as it is transformed into a flowering oasis.

Create a Robust, Permanent Green Roof

You will need: Impermeable sheeting cut to size, nails, weather-treated timber cut to size, L-shaped brackets, gravel, weed-control fabric, compost, perlite, and plants.
Tools: A hammer, a drill, and a trowel.

1. Cut a piece of impermeable sheeting so that it hangs slightly over the roof. Fasten it with a hammer and nails.

2. Construct a frame from 5–6 in. (12–15 cm) wide weather-treated timber to match the dimensions of your roof. Secure the corners with L-shaped brackets. Drill ½ in. (2 cm) drainage holes at the lower end if the roof is sloping, or at regular intervals all around if the roof is flat.

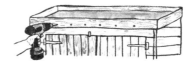

3. Pour a ½ to 1 in. (2–3 cm) layer of gravel into the frame. This will improve drainage and help reduce soil erosion. Cut a piece of weed-control membrane larger than the inside of the frame. Fix it to the frame with nails.

4. Fill the frame with compost mixed with perlite. The perlite will aid drainage and reduce the weight of the compost.

5. Plant varieties that don't grow too high and have shallow roots (see the suggestions on the next page). Water when needed, but be careful not to overwater.

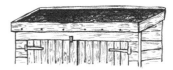

Six Plants for Green Roofs

Sedum

Go for small varieties like *Sedum rupestre, Sedum reflexum*, and *Sedum acre*, which will flower from June to August. Drought-resistant, they need little watering and will self-propagate.

Blue Fescue

A blue-green low-growing, clump-forming grass.

Sempervivum

Rosettes of spiky leaves that grow well in clusters on a sunny roof and need very little soil. Flowers from June to August.

Saxifrage

A low-growing, evergreen alpine plant. Pretty sprays of white flowers from May to June.

Creeping Thyme
Rich in nectars (insect-friendly!), and thrives in thin, well-drained soil. Flowers from May to August.

Thrift
Its natural environment is a cliff ledge, so the thrift will be hardy enough to survive on your roof. Pretty pink flowers too.

Easy Green Roofs

Buy a roll of living carpet made of coir, or fibers from the outer husk of a coconut, planted with sedum. This is bought by the square foot, which you cut to size to fit your roof. Lay a water-impermeable layer and a weed-control fabric first (some companies supply these with the turf), then roll out the carpet and water.

Green the City

All over our urban spaces there are patches of public land that have been neglected or abandoned. Whether it's a charmless roundabout, a relentlessly mowed roadside, or a neglected public flowerbed, each is bursting with the potential to come back to life.

The opportunity to cultivate uncared-for plots was seized in 1973 in New York by Liz Christy and her Green Guerrilla group. They planted vegetables on a derelict private lot and guerrilla gardening was born. Since then it has become an international movement, with organized groups stealthily planting and sowing at night, or more brazenly during the day. Although gardeners do not have legal rights to cultivate the land, many councils and governing bodies turn a blind eye to their activities and gradually, parched and boring scrubby land is greening up.

If urban rewilding appeals to you, look into events in your area (if you're based in New York City, check out greenguerillas.org). Alternatively, join in on International Sunflower Day (May 1), when guerrilla gardeners worldwide sow seeds of this cheerful plant in forgotten flowerbeds.

If you live on a tree-lined street, a modest guerrilla gardening project is planting up the forgotten ground around a tree (called a tree pit—see opposite or page 133). Pollinators and pedestrians will thank you for it.

How to Plant a Tree Pit

1. **Locate your pit.** Find one as close to your home as possible. Once planted, it will need some attention: occasional watering, weeding, removing litter, etc.

2. **Build a border around it.** This isn't essential but does help to protect the pit from wayward pedestrians and keeps the soil in one place. Construct a wooden frame from pieces of timber secured with L-shaped brackets at the corners.

3. **Pile on compost.** The earth around the tree is probably dry and depleted of nutrients. Give it a boost with organic matter such as garden, mushroom, or multi-purpose compost.

4. **Choose your plants.** Only the most robust will survive; they will have to contend with pollution, dog mess, and potential trampling by passersby. Small spring-flowering bulbs such as miniature daffodils, snowdrops, and dwarf irises will look pretty and are easy to grow. *Erigeron* (fleabane), a white daisy, survives most things and self-seeds in profusion. *Helianthus* (sunflower) can withstand neglect—choose a variety with small flowers—as can forget-me-nots. Ivy will look good all year round, and *Vinca* (periwinkle) and *Ajuga* (bugle) provide good ground cover. Grasses will also withstand most things.

5. **Water your plants.** Then wait to see what happens next.

Rebel Botanists

Plants that grow through pavement or in the crack of a wall
are often unloved and regarded as weeds to be discarded.
However, they can provide vital food for insects and birds.
A band of rebel botanists is on a mission to recognize and
respect these wild plants by naming them. Wherever they go,
they chalk the name of the plant on the ground or wall beside
it, then share the images on social media. The movement,
which began in France, has spread across Europe, and
although it's illegal to "deface" public property, most
councils turn a blind eye. One to try?

35

Refresh the Birds and the Bees

Like us, wildlife needs water to survive, but a supply can be
hard to find in urban environments, especially in the winter
when water is frozen or during hot summers when it can dry up
completely. Although birds have no sweat glands and need less
water than mammals, they do need to drink at least twice a day
and bathing is a vital part of their feather maintenance. Help
them out by providing a bird bath, either a ready-made one or
fashioned from an upturned trash can lid or similar. Keep it
topped up and clean it regularly. Alternatively, make a bee
drinker or build a mini pond.

Bee Drinker

Like all living creatures, bees and other pollinators need water. If the only option is a pond, they may drown trying to find it (this explains dead bees floating in outdoor swimming pools). What they need is a safe place to land and to drink. Here are three ways to provide one:

- Either drop a sponge into a bucket filled with water or hang a cloth over the rim with half of it submerged. This will create a wet landing platform for bees to drink from.

- Add a few pebbles to a bird bath or large pan of water to provide places for flying pollinators to land.

- Fill a saucer with water and add pebbles or marbles for bees to land on and drink from.

Mini Pond

A pond is a vital ingredient in any wildlife-friendly garden. It provides another drinking source and valuable habitat for multiple species. Any outdoor space, no matter how small, has room for one. All you need is a watertight container that is wide enough for wildlife to get in and out of easily. A large bowl, trash can lid, old ceramic sink, recycling box, or large plastic plant saucer will do nicely.

1. Find somewhere light but not in direct sun all day long. Either dig a hole and sink the container into it or place it on the ground.

2. Add a layer of gravel and stones of varying sizes. Place some near the edge so that wildlife can hop in and out easily.

3. Fill with rainwater.

4. Consider adding two or three aquatic plants, such as marsh marigold, water-crowfoot, or miniature water lily. They will oxygenate the water and provide food and shelter. Put the plants in aquatic baskets and fill with aquatic compost or a mix of sand and gravel. Top with gravel to keep them submerged.

5. Wait for the wildlife to arrive.

36

Love Roadside Wildflowers

It's easy to overlook the slivers of land that lie alongside roads,
or the barren grassy strips in the between busy highways.
Frequently neglected, strewn with litter, or scalped by mowers,
you may think there is little of interest to see. But stop to look
a closer and you may be surprised by what you find. Roadside
wildflowers feed and shelter bees, butterflies, birds, insects,
and other creatures, and are more valuable than ever before
as some wildflower dwelling species are in decline.

And many more species could thrive in these places, a fact that is increasingly being addressed by highway departments and local councils. In the United States, parkways in Texas, Virginia, and North Carolina are bursting into bloom as they are transformed into wildflower-rich habitats vital for species threatened by encroaching development.

One big change that would welcome more wildlife is to cut back on mowing—a more sustainable approach than sowing wildflower seeds. If grassy areas are left to grow, native species will return and seed, and wildlife will come. This "cut less, cut later" method is gradually being adopted by councils and highway authorities who can see the benefits it brings and the money it saves. Minnesota's Roadsides for Wildlife program prohibits mowing until after August, and the state of Florida has reduced its mowing to every six or eight weeks, rather than every three.

We all have to overcome the urge for neatness and embrace the unruly wild so our roadsides can flower and wildlife will flourish. One way to help make this happen is to petition your local governing bodies and ask what their policy is concerning roadside care. Suggest they mow less often and point out the financial benefits. Wait for a response and keep naggling until you get one!

Dig for Victory

Shopping in supermarkets, where the same fruit and vegetables are available all year round, can make us lose sight of seasonality. Growing your own produce, however, brings back a seasonal perspective. When you sow seeds in spring to harvest in summer or autumn, you become more aware of the passing year and the cycles of nature. This can be more important in the city, where we are at a distance from the natural world, than in the country, where it is all around. The other thing about producing your own food, of course, is that you get to eat it and you know where it comes from. No matter how small your space or how limited your time, there are ways to make this happen.

37

Be Your Own Herbalist

Everyone can grow herbs; all you need is a sunny windowsill, balcony, or doorstep. Having a few pots of leafy goodness lined up in a kitchen always feels good and can feel even better if you grow herbs that have a medicinal as well as a culinary purpose.

Until they were replaced with synthetic products in the nineteenth century, herbs were the principal ingredient of medicinal practice. Advances in medicine have largely made them redundant, and it is unwise to self-medicate—a general practitioner or qualified herbalist should be your first port of call—but they can be effective when used for minor ailments.

To get a real understanding of the range and efficacy of medicinal herbs, visit a physic garden, where you will find them growing in orderly, helpfully labeled groups.

Six Healing Herbs

Chamomile (*Anthemis nobilis*)
Infuse the pretty flowers in boiling water
and drink as a tea to ease insomnia and
soothe the nerves. Used in moderation,
this will also settle troubled stomachs.

Fennel (*Foeniculum vulgare*)
The fronds of fennel grow to significant
heights (around 3 ft or 1 m), so this is best
grown outdoors rather than on a windowsill.
Let it flower and go to seed, then infuse
one teaspoon of seeds in a cup of hot water
to relieve stomach cramps. When chewed,
fennel seeds can also settle the stomach after
a rich meal (you may have eaten them in an
Indian restaurant in a sugar coating).

Feverfew (*Tanacetum parthenium*)
Known as "the medieval aspirin,"
the fresh leaves of this daisy-like plant
can ease headaches, migraines, and
period pain. Eat with a piece of bread
to disguise its bitter flavor.

Lemon Balm (*Melissa officinalis*)
When boiled in hot water for tea, lemon
balm is a mild antidepressant and sedative
that helps the nervous system.

Rosemary (*Rosmarinus officinalis*)
Tea made from fresh rosemary helps
stimulate memory and, when consumed
in moderation, can ease a hangover.

Lavender (*Lavandula*)
The soothing scent of lavender is
a tonic for the nervous system and
helps insomnia. Collect flower heads
before drying and putting them
in a cotton sachet to place under
a pillow, or run them under the
tap when drawing a bath.

Tips for Growing Herbs in Pots

• Make sure your pots have drainage holes. Herbs hate
sitting in damp soil. Place the pot on a drainage saucer so
that water doesn't leak over your table top if growing indoors.

• Not all herbs need the same conditions but most need
plenty of sunlight. Place by a south-facing window if possible.

• Don't overwater, just dampen the soil with room
temperature water when it has dried out.

• Fill the pots with well-drained soil by adding 25 percent
perlite or grit to a loam-based compost.

Create a Container Garden

Shortage of space does not need to prevent you from growing your own produce. Anyone can plant a hanging basket with tumbling cherry tomatoes or strawberries, or grow a little fruit tree in a pot. Lettuces grow readily in a container as long as they are kept watered, and are a fraction of the price of bagged supermarket varieties.

To cultivate a one-pot allotment, fill a container—the bigger the better—with soil rich in organic matter. Find the sunniest spot in your garden or backyard (this is important—vegetables will only thrive if they get a decent amount of sunlight), then choose what to grow. Either sow seeds, paying attention to instructions on the packet or, for a head start, use seedlings, which will be ready to go.

Grow your vegetables in rows and mix different leaf shapes and forms to create a crop that is attractive as well as nourishing. You could also add a few edible flowering plants (marigolds, nasturtium, and borage, for example) to give your container garden a colorful vibe.

Mini Vegetables

A good option when space is limited. Try sowing seeds of baby broccoli (broccolini), baby beetroot, dwarf kale, mini cauliflower, or finger carrots. They make attractive little plants, and their small size doesn't mean they have little flavor—if anything, it is more intense. Sow in batches in spring and repeat to keep the crops coming.

Dwarf Varieties

These produce normal-sized vegetables but grow on smaller plants. Non-climbing dwarf runner beans, for example, are great in pots, as are dwarf patio raspberries, which have thornless stems and plenty of fruit.

Climbing Plants

Some vegetables are happiest clambering upwards and will grow in a deep pot with some sort of support, such as a trellis against a wall. Try cucumbers, beans, and squash, but go for dwarf varieties as standard sizes will soon overwhelm any structure. A vertical structure in your garden will also add height and visual interest. Plant low growing lettuces to maximize the space.

39

Raise Chickens

There are more and more chicken keepers in the city today, and it's easy to see why. Finding a freshly laid egg or two in the coop every morning is a cheering, and soon-to-be delicious, treat. Hens are also amusing and relatively carefree creatures to have around. Like all animals, however, they need to be properly cared for and there are a number of things to consider before you embark on the path to becoming a city poultry keeper.

Have I got enough space?
Although chickens don't need masses of space, they don't like to be too confined. In their perfect world, they would free range in the garden all day, pecking at the ground and scuffing it up with their feet. You will need a hen house with a nesting box and an enclosed run, at least three feet (1 sq. m) per hen, but seven square feet (2 sq. m) or more is preferable. If you have room, section off an area of the garden with netting so you can let them out to roam and keep your plants safe (they peck at everything).

How many should I get?
Chickens are sociable creatures and like to go around in gangs, so get more than one: three is a good number for a small space. If you are getting chickens for eggs (not for meat or to raise more chickens), you will need hens. Avoid cockerels unless you want your hens to have chicks.

Do I have enough time to look after them?
Although chickens are fairly resilient creatures, consider the time and care you'll be able to provide for a flock of your own birds. They will need to be let out of their coop every morning and herded back into their shelter as soon as it gets dark to keep them safe from predators. Throughout the day, you will need to keep an eye on the chicken feeder (which dispenses food pellets throughout the day) and ensure their water is clean and filled to the top.

How do I keep them healthy?
Like any animal, chickens can get ill. A few precautionary measures make this less likely. Ensure they have worming and lice/mite treatments, keep their coop clean and dry, provide regular food and clean water and they will be fine.

40

Grow Microgreens

Even if you have no outside space at all, you can grow a nourishing and tasty crop on your windowsill. Microgreens are the seedlings of vegetables and herbs, harvested when the first leaves appear. Their flavor is intense and they look really pretty, which is why they have become so popular with chefs, who sprinkle them all over their dishes.

Most vegetables can be grown as microgreens. The purple stems of beetroot, red cabbage, and radish look especially good scattered over salads and soups, and herbs such as cilantro and basil cropped as microgreens pack a mighty flavor. You could also try broccoli, cauliflower, kale, fennel ... the list is endless.

Once picked, microgreens lose their flavor and color quickly, which is why supermarkets rarely stock them— another good reason to grow them yourself.

BASIL

ARUGULA

SWISS CHARD

BEETROOT

MUSTARD GREENS

How to Grow Microgreens

You will need: Vegetable or herb seeds, organic potting soil,
a seed tray or any small plastic container (a takeaway box or a
disposable plate will do) with holes in the bottom for drainage,
a plant mister, and a spoon.

1. Fill the seed tray with 2–4 in. (5–10 cm) soil.
Flatten lightly with the back of a spoon.

2. Scatter the seeds thickly and evenly over the soil.
Press gently into the soil with your hand or the back
of a spoon so they make contact.

3. Scatter a layer of soil over the seeds.

4. Dampen the surface with a plant mister. You need a
light touch when it comes to watering microgreens: too much
water will dislodge the seeds and wash them away.

5. Place on a warm, sunny windowsill.

6. Once the seeds have sprouted, which will be in less
than a month, continue spraying with the plant mister.

7. When the first set of leaves appear and the plant is about
2 in. (5 cm) tall, snip off the shoots with a pair of scissors.

8. Wash and pat dry with a kitchen towel. Serve at once for
the best flavor. You could store the remainder in the
fridge, but don't leave them for long.

Plant a Mini Orchard

The dream of having an orchard isn't necessarily out of reach for the urban dweller. If you have any outdoor space, you can grow fruit trees. It is said that five trees make an orchard, but just one or two carefully chosen ones can deliver blossoms in spring and abundant fruit in autumn.

A couple of things to keep in mind: if you are growing just one or two apple trees, choose self-pollinating varieties and prune your trees regularly, otherwise they will grow too big. If you are planting several trees, choose a mixture of early- and late-harvest varieties to spread out your harvest.

A Dwarf Tree in a Big Container

Many fruit trees, including apple and pear varieties, are grafted onto dwarfing rootstocks. This reduces their size, making them easier to fit into a small space and to manage. Plant in a generously sized container and you can turn your patio or yard into a productive growing space. Just remember to water regularly and plant in high-quality, well-drained soil.

Grow at an Angle: Cordon Trees

Perfect for small gardens, cordons (usually apples and pears) have single stems with short side shoots, which bear the fruit. They are usually planted at a 45-degree angle as this is more productive, although they can also be grown vertically. Cordons need to be trained against a wall or fence and planted in a sheltered, well-drained spot. Choose a dwarfing rootstock to keep them small and tidy (look for G11 or G30 rootstock. G30 is particularly well-suited for North American climates), and plant in winter. Prune in August by cutting back new side shoots to three leaves. When the leading shoot reaches the maximum height for your space, prune it back.

Grow Against the Wall: Espalier Trees

Grown on dwarfing rootstock, espaliers have their lateral branches trained to grow horizontally. This encourages them to grow out rather than up, making them ideal for small spaces. Buy an espaliered tree and maintain its shape as it grows by regular pruning. Think beyond apples and pears—plums, peaches, cherries, and apricots can all be grown as espaliers.

How to Plant Your Tree

1. Soak the root ball of the tree for at least ten minutes.

2. Dig a hole double the size of the root ball.

3. Stand the tree in the hole, making sure the graft (where the stem bulges) is above the ground.

4. Fill in the space surrounding the root ball of the tree.

5. Tie branches of cordons and espaliers to securely fastened wire supports with garden twine. Tie fruit trees in containers to a stake with a tree tie or an old pair of tights.

6. Water thoroughly and continue to water once a week during the first growing season, or more during dry weather.

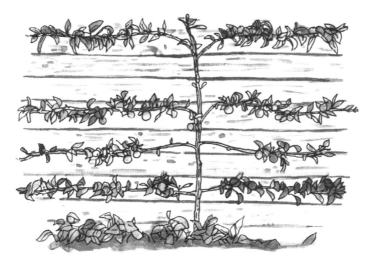

Find Your Wild Tribe

Sometimes the urban nature warrior can't do it alone. Certain projects require a coming together of like-minded folks to make things happen. Find an initiative that piques your interests— a tree-planting program, say, or a conservation taskforce—and pitch in. Working with others, and with nature, is a great way to make a real difference in your community. Plus, you get to meet lots of new people and learn new skills. If you can't find a group or project that matches your interests, start one yourself. Little beats the power of a community working together to get things done. Nature will thank you for it!

42

Take a City Hike

For most of us, most of the time, walking in the city is all about getting somewhere. We hurry between the station and the office on our commute, or dash to the shops or to meet friends. "Walking" as an activity is thought of as a country pursuit. However, there are many opportunities for a proper walk in towns and cities, many through leafy, wildlife- and wildflower-rich stretches. Here are some places to consider.

Along a Disused Railway Line

The most famous example of a repurposed railway line is the High Line in Manhattan, New York, which stretches for over a mile above the city along a section of the former railroad. With plants of all colors and textures along its length, the High Line is a welcome respite from the commotion below. In London, England, the Parkland Walk follows the route of a closed railway line to the top of a hill at Alexandra Palace and boasts birds, bats, and wildflowers. There may be a disused railway line near you. Take a look and find out.

A Guided Walking Tour

Become a tourist in your own town or city for a day and find a nature-focused guided tour. A walk in the company of a wildlife expert, ornithologist, or urban forager will reveal many surprising and previously unknown observations.

A Walking Group

Link up with other nature enthusiasts for regular walks.
Canals, riverbanks, and city squares are all wildlife-rich destinations.
Alternatively, take public transport beyond the city limits and spend a
day walking in a leafy suburb or woodland, with a pit stop for lunch.

Explore Your Local Park

Spend time really getting to know a nearby park, going beyond your
usual places. Walk its boundaries, explore its nooks and crannies,
and map its wildlife. Then treat yourself to a cup of coffee and
pastry at the neighborhood café.

43

Join the Hive

There has never been a better time to keep bees. The numbers of these essential pollinators may be declining, but a growing urban beekeeping movement means that we all have a chance to help them recover. The city is, counter-intuitively, a perfect habitat for bees. Warmer temperatures, a variety of plant material, and fewer pesticides mean that urban bees flourish, often producing more honey than their country cousins. The only problem they face is insufficient pollen due to the large number of urban beekeepers, so if you do decide to become an urban apiarist, plant some bee-friendly plants near the hive if possible to keep them going.

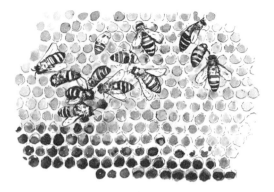

Setting up a hive yourself is quite an undertaking, however, requiring considerable time, equipment, and knowledge. Fortunately, there are other ways to do it.

- **Ask at work.** Many businesses now have hives on their roofs and run programs to involve employees in their upkeep. Your company may have one in place already. If it doesn't, now could be the time to rally colleagues and set one up.

- **Find a local beekeepers' association.** Most cities will have at least one. Join up and pitch in to get advice on setting up on your own, or help others maintain their hives.

- **Start a community beehive.** Find a group of committed would-be beekeepers (a community garden is a good place to start looking), a location, and a local beekeeper willing to guide the project and take it from there.

- **Adopt a hive.** Some beekeepers have too many hives for their space and will pay you monthly rent to install one in your garden, visit a few times a year to keep an eye on things, and share the honey with you.

- **Sponsor a hive.** A totally hands-off method of beekeeping. You pay a subscription and in return get regular news updates and a share of the honey.

44

Help a Wildlife Shelter

If you've ever come across an injured bird or animal, you
will know how helpless that can make you feel. The urge to
take it home and care for it is a strong one but can also be fatal
for the creature, unless you really know what you are doing.
Fortunately, there are wildlife rehabilitation centers in most
cities, which will look after injured wild animals and advise you
on their best care. Most of these centers depend on volunteers
to keep them running—a great opportunity to do your part
for the animals that share our urban environment.

These centers exist because encroaching development has meant that the amount of habitat available for wildlife has been reduced. Small mammals and birds have adapted to survive but this is not always successful. Their encounters with human activity can lead to injury and death, caused unintentionally by us. Urban wildlife rehabilitation centers aim to help heal this damage by caring for sick, orphaned, and injured wild animals. Once the animals are fully fit and healthy, they are released back into the (urban) wild.

How You Can Help

Many of these shelters have volunteer programs where you can work alongside the professional veterinary staff on various tasks. Duties could involve collecting injured migratory birds, monitoring duck nests, handling animals for examination, hand-feeding baby birds, and cleaning enclosures. The greatest need for volunteers is in the spring and summer, when newborn animals are most vulnerable. Creatures you may encounter (although this varies from region to region and country to country) include injured foxes, hedgehogs, badgers, owls, ducks, bats, wild birds, and squirrels.

45

Adopt or Plant a City Tree

Urban environments without trees are desolate, lifeless places.
A tree-lined street, an arbor in a city square, or a grove in a park,
on the other hand, is a welcome burst of nature. There is no
end to the benefits trees bring. They offer shade in the summer,
provide a habitat for birds and insects, reduce pollution,
and lessen the effects of climate change (which causes higher
temperatures in summer and wetter winters).

Although plenty of cities worldwide are actively engaged in
planting trees, many trees disappear through aging, disease, or as
a result of human activity. There is always room for more trees.

Be a Tree Warrior

- Tampa, Florida is the world leader for urban trees. According to calculations by the Senseable City Lab at the Massachusetts Institute of Technology, more than one third of the city is given over to tree cover.

- Other cities with a high percentage of tree cover include Singapore, Oslo, Sydney, Cambridge, MA, and Vancouver.

- The Arbor Day Foundation (arborday.org) runs the Time for Trees initiative, with more than 3,400 registered communities helping to reduce air pollution by planting trees.

- If you don't have time to get involved with tree planting, consider donating toward tree planting instead by giving someone the gift of a tree through Trees for Change (treesforachange.com) which offers a certificate in return for your green gift.

46

Become a Plant Hunter

Tread in the footsteps of the great plant collectors by visiting a botanical garden. A wonderful mix of science, history, conservation, and horticulture, there are around 1,800 botanical gardens worldwide, with 550 in Europe and 200 in North America. They are a great place to wander and wonder. Many have special collections of plants, such as alpines, tropical plants, cacti, and orchids, housed in architecturally splendid greenhouses at different temperatures and conditions.

We are in danger of losing many plant species because of climate change, habitat destruction, and farming practices. Now, more than ever, as plant conservation becomes a priority, it is incredibly important to support botanical gardens. As well as undertaking botanical research, they keep databases of rare or endangered plants as living collections, often with the intention of reintroducing them into their original habitats. Usually run by universities or scientific organizations, botanical gardens often maintain seed banks, cataloging and storing seeds from plants that are rare or threatened with extinction.

Botanical gardens are not dry and dusty places, however. They are living, breathing gardens. Themed exhibitions are held to complement the collections of plants, and you will also discover herb gardens and arboretums of rare and unusual trees.

Grow a Community Garden

Living in a built-up environment without any outdoor space makes it difficult to grow your own food. Little is as satisfying as planting and tending to fruit and vegetables that you can then harvest, cook, and eat. Community gardens answer this need by providing space to do exactly that.

Easier to join than an allotment program (which often has a long waiting list), community gardens are usually created on uncared-for, scruffy patches of land and funded by local councils or charities, offering a place to cultivate your very own crops.

Although not huge (a square raised bed per gardener is the norm), community gardens are big enough to grow a surprisingly abundant supply of produce. They also plug you into the local community, improve the place you live, and attract wildlife. Depending on the size and liveliness of the garden, you could find yourself learning about compost, planting bee-friendly flowerbeds, pruning fruit trees, sharing seeds, and enjoying the company and plant knowledge of the other gardeners.

Community Orchards

A growing number of community orchards are also springing up and offer the opportunity to work with others to produce and harvest apples and pears. In addition to the joy of growing fruit, there is also the deliciousness of the juice to savor. Fall harvest is often a time for celebration, and you may find a cider or fall festival in your area.

Make It Happen

Wherever there is a scruffy patch of land, there is the potential for a community garden, a few fruit trees, or both. If you can't find one near you, think about gathering some like-minded people and starting your own. You never know where it may lead.

48

Become a City Farmer

Chances are that you don't have enough space to look after
a flock of sheep, a couple of donkeys, or a few goats (although
you may have space for chickens; see page 116). Fortunately,
there are places that do. Urban farming is gathering momentum
as farming techniques are adapted to built-up environments.
These city farms, often spanning several acres, give you the
chance to see animals that are normally only spotted in the
countryside. Besides sheep, donkeys, and goats, you might meet
pigs, geese, llamas, ducks, and rare-breed chickens.

Much of the income needed to run a city farm is dependent on visitors. At petting farms, children learn farm-based skills by getting up close to animals, feeding newborn lambs or scratching a pig behind the ears. Other farms have riding schools or offer courses to learn skills such as beekeeping or spinning wool. Some have convivial cafés so you can enjoy coffee and cake to the accompaniment of a variety of clucks, squawks, and honks.

How You Can Help

Volunteers are often needed to help keep these places going. Most do not receive government funding and are run by charities or community groups. Sign up and soon you could be helping out at lambing time, feeding the donkeys, or clearing out the hen house. It is a wonderful way to learn about animals, escape from the city, dabble in rural life, and generally de-stress.

49

Create and Share an Urban Nature Map

Although the urban landscape is largely cultivated, patches of wilderness still exist. Often overlooked and left alone, these areas provide vital habitats for wildlife and wildflowers. One of the best ways to locate them and record what you find is to do a spot of wildlife cartography. Creating an urban nature map is a useful tool, not just for the wildlife spotter but, potentially, for developers, planners, and conservation groups who could use the valuable information you have gathered to create more habitats and avoid destroying what already exists.

How to Map Your Natural Environment

1. Find a good-quality, large-scale map of your local area, ideally with a scale of two miles to one inch.

2. With a pencil, outline the best remaining areas of natural habitats—woodland, wetland, parks, nature reserves, etc.—that you can find.

3. Color them in.

4. Look for smaller areas of habitats: a few trees, a leafy square, a strip of land beside a canal or river. Outline them with a pencil, then color them in with a different colour. These corridors connect wildlife to the larger areas.

5. Choose an area you have plotted and go and visit it.

6. Record what you find there: insects, birds, and wildflowers.

7. Add drawings or photographs of your findings to the map in the relevant places.

8. Share your findings on social media and ask others to contribute their findings to your map.

Help Restore Natural Habitats

The semi-rural areas around towns and cities are essential habitats for wildlife. The taller grasses surrounding a golf course could bloom with wildflowers for bees. The grubby canal and its towpath could be where a duck builds its nest, and former industrial and landfill sites may be home to stag beetles and woodpeckers. While many of these areas are best left to nature to "rewild," some could be given a hand. Look for conservation projects near you and join in.

Remove invasive plant species: Once certain plants establish, they muscle out everything else, creating a monoculture. Volunteer to help remove invasive species such as purple loosestrife, Japanese honeysuckle, and kudzu.

Clear waterways: Any water in an urban environment is important for aquatic animals and birds. Many waterways, however, are polluted and put wildlife at risk. Volunteer for a canal or river clear-out to ease the damage created.

Look after bats: Bats often hang out in cities, roosting in abandoned buildings where they aren't disturbed. Join a bat-monitoring program and help survey bat populations. Then use the information gathered to create habitats that will encourage more bats to roost in the area.

Help manage woodland: A number of cities are lucky to have areas of woodland, some with ancient trees, situated along their streets. These precious places need looking after and most have a volunteer program to do this. Sign up and you could learn how to plant and prune street trees or harvest and propagate native seed.

Create a wildflower meadow: The best way to encourage pollinators is to provide nectar-rich plants for them to feed on. A meadow of carefully chosen flowering plants, perhaps on a roundabout or neglected flowerbed, is a good way to do this.